THE HOME STRAIGHT

Truffle books

For we live in webs of kinship and friendship
fragile as a spider's work and as easily torn

THE HOME STRAIGHT

John Comino-James

CONTENTS

Benedictions	6
Afterwards	8
On the way here	10
Luz	13
Prime numbers	14
Mapo Turístico	16
Those evenings of holiday slides	18
The journey	22
Once in short trousers	24
Just landed safely in Rhodes	26
Peacocks, goats and sandalwood	28
One morning in Holy Week	30
Visiting family graves	31
The tower	34
At the corner of Padre Varela	36
On the way down to Jericho	37
I must have wanted	38
One thousand pieces	40
The home straight	42

BENEDICTIONS
In memory of Phyllis Mary James

Why, as a child, was I shown
the brook you paddled in?
Sullen I shrank in the back of the car
uninterested in the fields and farms
where you grew up: why should I grasp
the novel risk of a plumbed-in inside bath
and electric light from an engine in the shed?

Blackberries I ate, and tractors I could name
but cow parsley, willowherb.
hips, haws, and teasels.
herb-Robert, yarrow, thrift and
old man's beard meant nothing at all
to the boy with a Meccano set.
Rooks building high in the elms
were a sign, you said ....

Now you are everywhere and nowhere.

Too late, too late for you to see,
Galanthus elwesii multiply
Prunus subhirtella autumnalis
lofts an arch of pink for days of grey Christmas.
Metasequoia glyptostroboides bought pot-bound
as a bargain is finally growing away,
Pinus wallichiana and *Quercus rubra*
are almost climbable towers.

Half a dozen cyclamen
(They'll do well under that pine, you said)
spread slowly year on year,
accumulate like interest.
Hamamelis mollis won't grow for me
but the Myrtle and a Beauty Bush do well.
and *Parrotia Persica* colours up nicely ...

You would have loved to have a nursery,
you told me once, would have loved
to grow plants for a living.
Now at the end of the yard
pale soft-scented *Lonicera fragrantissima*
startles in January sunlight.

and you, you are everywhere and nowhere,
nowhere, nowhere and everywhere.

AFTERWARDS

What would happen afterwards
was quite easily decided,

no question of a do in a posh hotel
or a bit of a spread in the village hall;

we just borrowed a couple of kettles
and invited everyone back to the house

for sausage rolls and supermarket quiche,
Victoria sponge and Mr Kipling cakes

and tried to make everyone welcome.
The sombre mood lifted bit by bit

as strangers introduced themselves
and the relief of a *Do you remember..?*

cautiously opened the laughter
while beyond the picture window

her garden was lit by hellebores,
crocuses and early daffs.

There were scattered cushions of heather
and someone from the flower club said

She was always pinching cuttings!
I remember her getting that dogwood!

She'd have loved to see such friendship
gathered in the room she'd not long left;

You won't know me, but we sang in the choir
and *She taught my boys in Infant School*

till finally *We'd best be getting on our way*
and the shaken hand, *She had a wonderful life*

the awkward kiss on the cheek, *Hard as it is,*
she went the kindest way that anyone can go.

The door latch fell some fifteen years ago
but what comes back is not a mourning-day

of prayers and hymns – no, time restores instead
an afternoon of gifts, of story-stitchers

weaving her truest shroud, their patchwork
of memory, invisible, rich, collected and collective:

unfurled and briefly shown,
too broad, too various. too precious,

and itself too transient for any one of us to keep
or hope to hold entire, or know.

ON THE WAY HERE

I

Coming down a slope before the road turned,
I saw there was a church-tower off to the left
square among trees at the end of a field
sharpened by low-angled sun
like a moment of another time
a time before combines and tractors
a time of sheaves on the tines of pitchforks
and my one grandfather repairing hay rakes in his forge
and the other using horses to bring the harvest in
and neither one knowing the other.

II

I saw a photograph from those times once,
no-one that they knew, just someone I met,
a chap who used to drive a traction engine round
the farms at threshing time. He was wearing a suit
and on the back in awkward script it said
taking in the photographers clothes.

I always smiled at the thought of the man
behind the camera bending forward under a black cloth
half undressed with his socks held up by suspenders
but now I wonder if he carried outfits with him
so clients could choose how they looked
for mothers wives and sweethearts.

III

For choosing how you looked was important
in the days when having your likeness taken
was a special event wherever it was, whether outdoors
or in a studio with a wall of windows facing north
and a camera with bellows on a mahogany stand,
a Dallmeyer lens in a brass tube
and someone in collar tie and waistcoat
gripping a rubber bulb and counting off
the seconds of exposure.

For choosing how you looked was important
and arranging how you looked
was important for others
to be able to remember you and explain who you were
and I think of all those men in uniform
ethereally inverted on ground glass
asked to *Hold* before the *Thank you Sir*,
those fathers sweethearts uncles brothers sons
so well turned out before the train to France
and I think of those who 'had his father's eyes'
and I think of that generation's new-born man-child face
being washed, its nostrils cleared of mucus
its upper lip wiped clean of birth-slime
where the soft moustache would come,
and its cry from lungs that would savour a Woodbine
or choke on mustard gas.

III

And on the way here I saw sunlight
catch a church-tower square among trees
and just for a moment I thought I saw
at the end of a field
the brasses' flash as horses turned, spilling
their animal stench back over the plough
but the road took suddenly
a tightening bend to the right and nearly caught me out --
but I got it together and swept on,
past the stone memorial weathered on the green.

LUZ

In the street called light
a man dreaming of elsewhere
treads on his shadow

PRIME NUMBERS
In memory of Andrew James

Rain chatters on glass
in ill-fitting windows: water settles
on the ridge-and-furrow field.

Behind the curtains,
gusts rattle a sash: I sense the outside
breathing out and breathing in.

Insomnia gnaws.
The house becomes a skull, brick mortar bone.
Along the lane sheep huddle

where pasture rises.
Why not shepherd them in from the field's edge
to the brain's fold, count them, one

two, three, believing
the discipline will ease the restive mind
but both two and three are prime

and five is the next,
the day of your birth, then seven, eleven
till thirteen times five

are the years you lived,
and I imagine a family lunch
where you and I are playing

a game taking turns
to call out the next prime number
between one and a hundred

without hesitation.
Between sixty-one and sixty-seven
I falter. *Fibonnacci!*

you cry: I counter
Fermat! and everyone laughs, not knowing
I'm winging it, dropping names

to get by while you
could explain the Sieve of Eratosthenes
without batting an eye....

still sleep avoids me
and darkness thins behind the window glass.
My imaginary game

plays out the magic
of its spell, turning absence into presence:
when the table is cleared,

glasses polished, cruet
put away, we stand looking out, watching kites
circle in a Sunday sky.

MAPO TURÍSTICO

So too in that city, a taxonomy of streets:
Callejon, alleyway; *Calle,* street;
Avenida, avenue:
and the untranslatable *Calzada.*

And in their names, commemorations,
declensions of history,
Saints, Bishops, Generals –
Francisco, Compostela, Lacret –
which a little research will explain.
Agua Dulce, Amenidad, Amistad –
Dolores, Flores, and *Fuentes.*
Virtudes, Posible, and *Milagros* …
Sweet Water, Pleasantness, Friendship…

But better perhaps to explore leaving
the dictionary behind you,
stepping out of your shadow
or into your shadow
ready for a miracle.

Let *Espada* be sword or long-dead bishop
and never mind which.
Say *Luz* never light
Vapor never steam
and *Sol* never sun.
Avoid the bustle of footsteps in *Soledad*
holding your own solitude inviolate

Maybe the best municipal intentions shook
these names like tinsel in a kaleidoscope:
this is how they fell.

But one long road, *Enamorados*,
a passage for those who've found eachother,
that one detaches itself from the map,
floats free, escapes its borders,
and passes everywhere.

THOSE EVENINGS OF HOLIDAY SLIDES
In memory of Howell Charles Morris

I

I should remember the pictures better,
but what comes to mind
is how the slides came back from Hemel Hempstead

in little yellow boxes with self-addressed labels,
and the old Gnome projector with its fragile lamp
in its leatherette case, the glass beaded screen

and the neighbours coming in for coffee and biscuits
to get first hand news of places
they'd only read about in magazines.

Going abroad was a novelty back then,
not many people did it and nobody flew
and you couldn't take much cash:

so nearly every year in a darkened room
I heard about French trains with slatted wooden seats
and *The most enormous engines that you've ever seen*

or waking up in Basel in the *wagon lit*
to fresh croissants on the station and those funny toilets
which are only a hole but do have places for your feet.

The tours took in Austria, Switzerland, the Italian lakes.
and the pictures, taken with a Kodak Retinette,
were mostly views: *This was our hotel,*

right on the water. Everywhere's so clean
and *There are mountain flowers everywhere.*
you've never seen so many, and *The cows have bells*

that you can hear from miles away.
These are some chalets that we saw. Every morning
they open their windows and hang their bedding out to air.

We'd all hear how the coach had to reverse
to make it round some terrible hairpin high up in the alps
and the drop you couldn't bear to look at –

Some driving, that! And this is the lovely couple we met
in Venice where we saw the Doge's palace.
The courier was wonderful, could not have been more ...

I never asked why they never went on to Ravenna
to visit the grave of my cousin killed
at Comacchio just as the war was coming to an end

but they did tell everyone they saw where Mussolini
was strung up along with Clara Petacci and a few others:
that must have been really important to them.

II

I remember other pictures better;
two photographs in black and white, more real, in frames.
Howell my cousin with the big drum in the OTC at school

and one, much later, in the Commandos,
sporting a fine moustache, striding in uniform
towards the camera in a street somewhere

just around a corner of my childhood.
They always said that as he was training at Guy's
he didn't have to join up, but he chose to go.

III

For years I imagined Comacchio
as being like one of those lakes on the holiday slides

where you might get down from a coach and look across
a picturesque expanse of water surrounded by pasture

but then for no particular reason one afternoon,
I Googled Comacchio and up came Operation Roast,

an assault across a brackish lagoon with a muddy shore
where the amphibious Weasels got bogged down

and commandos thigh deep in water had to manhandle
their storm boats and Goatleys across the shallows

before they could engage the outboard motors.
About twelve hundred Germans held a spit of land

between the inland water and the open sea, I read,
and the British objectives had rather incongruous biblical names,

Peter, Isiah, Amos, Ezra and Leviticus. Looking at the map,
you'd have been going to Leviticus to clear kill or capture.

I imagine your boots webbing battledress filthy with slime
but those are only words, just as fear adrenaline

courage and exhaustion are different words
just as grenade sten and bayonet are also different words...

And, cousin-that-I-never-met, you haunt me still,
more than any of our cousins that I know or knew.

Among numberless battalions of sacrificed slaughtered changed
or dispossessed, you are my own familiar, my own mid-century ghost

and when I speak of you, I'll say as I have always said
He was killed at Lake Comacchio, just as the war was ending,

and inwardly reflect *You would have been a healer, you who learned to kill*
and promise once again I'll never use of you those easy words, *He fell.*

THE JOURNEY

When we made those day-long journeys into Wales
the car went in for service a day or two before:
oil and water, battery and tires,
the carburetor tuned, points checked,
suspension greased, plugs cleaned.
Running sweet as a nut, the garage-man said.

We got the house prepared
for a three-week absence:
water off at the main,
electric off at the meter,
the gates shut firmly behind us.
The buddleia would flower for passers-by.

Inside my head my father still recites the route,
Bristol Gloucester Ross; Monmouth Raglan.
Abergavenny Crickhowell. Bwlch.
Brecon then *Trecastle.*
Llandovery Llandeilo Carmarthen
and finally into St Clears.

Llanddowror Llanteg.
Not so far now, mum would say
as we went through Kilgetty,
We'll be there quite soon
and soon would be Tenby.
Castle Hill and Goscar Rock.

I understand it now.
I thought we were going away,
but dad was only ever going home,
deep into Pembrokeshire.
Little England beyond Wales he always said
though you couldn't say that now.

I understand it now.
I thought he was driving our Riley,
but his old BSA was the car he was steering,
retracing those overnight journeys
with the windscreen flat on the bonnet,
before the war, when the roads were empty...

I would like to remember more
but all I recall are the names
of places we never actually stopped at.
On the winding ribbon of the road,
towns were unfortunate knots.
They should bypass this, mum said

and now it's not the road we used to follow,
not yard by yard or mile by mile.
We saw the first roundabouts and ring roads,
crawler lanes and double white lines.
the Bailey Bridge at Carmarthen...
In any case we take the motorway now

stopping at one of the services.
But when I say: *Magor, Cardiff Gate;
Sarn Park,* even *Pont Abraham* --
somehow the magic has gone.
Toilets and diesel. Just a quick stop.
Muffins or fries. And the urge to press on.

ONCE IN SHORT TROUSERS

I used to know how things worked,
had Newnes Pictorial Knowledge
with cutaway fold-outs and
the Observer Books of Aircraft and Butterflies:
the DH110 and Silver Washed Fritillary.

Tommy Walls used the morse code.
Dan Dare fought with Sondar at his side
and the Mekon floated like a frog on a lily pad.
Luck of the Legion stormed desert forts
And my balsa-wood gliders soared out of Colditz.

My bike had Sturmey Archer three-speed gears.
Lucas lit me homeward, fractions in my satchel:
divide Algebra by Latin, put Hall and Knight
over Hillard and Botting,
determine the square root of schooldays.

Butterflies clouded the holiday fields:
Never take more than one egg from a nest,
they warned us. Tadpoles in jam jars
turned into frogs. You changed the needle
in the gramophone to play those 78s.

Innocence was safe as a Meccano set,
a No 1 Clockwork motor
powered a dragline dredger
or transporter bridge..
It's a marvel how he does it,
Grandmother said.

Filaments glowed, visible through slots
in the fibre-board back of the wireless.
You needed aerial and earth
to get Two Way Family Favourites
and the nine o' clock news.

With screwdriver and soldering iron
and Scroggie's Foundations of Wireless
I understood triode valves and superhet receivers:
my cathode-ray oscilloscope
displayed Lissajous figures.

Now in touch-screen land
I finger the icon, scroll down the pop-up menu,
tap 'show invisibles', follow the hyperlinks
to search the never-was-it-ever of the past
looking for sticklebacks in ditches.

The Fairey Gannet had contra-rotating propellers.
Have you seen a grasshopper lately?
It's all there somewhere, behind this glass.
Is there a password that opens the land of before?
The log-in window mocks and shudders: *Nevermore.*

JUST LANDED SAFELY IN RHODES
In memory of Andrew James

I

Acres of forest were felled
for gutta percha to insulate submarine cables,
to enable the pulse of telegraphy in undersea corridors of copper.

In the age of the satellite phone,
who remembers the need to book a Christmas day call
to Australia? The echoes and delays on the line

as remote now from everyday experience
as semaphore arms or heliographs,
as Aldis lamps, talking drums or messengers over the mountains.

Once, in a certain kind of school, boys in short trousers
dipped pens into china inkwells, translated
the story of Philíppedes, writing in a fair hand:

and somewhere, in a private collection,
Luc Olivier Merson's *Le Soldat de Marathon*
collapses naked against a background of unlikely crenellations,

while longbeards fling up their arms in relief
and a young woman turns away aghast,
apparently confused by such a fine physique.

II

Palm leaves burning on the beach
call signal fires to mind: the Knights of St John
had their early-warning system of watchtowers
and fortified outposts, of look-outs
scanning the sea for an enemy's fleet.

Radar, developed for military needs,
tracks the seasonal migration of holiday flights
and taxi-drivers recognise each airline's livery.
Passengers stepping from cabin climate
into the kerosene heat of the airport apron

switch on their mobiles, restore the umbilical tether
to a system that tracks their every move.
Baggage conveyors rumble.
From masts like those on Monte Smith
packets of data pulse for home,

Just landed safely in Rhodes.

PEACOCKS, GOATS AND SANDALWOOD
In memory of Richard Jeans

I

Never far from the sea
       on what Auden called *a lake turned inside out*

Never far from the sea
       that swallowed Icarus, doomed flier

Never far from the sea
       that witches navigate in sieves

Never far from the sea,
       the horizon scanned
       for flares, funnel-smoke, white sails.
       Ariadne weeps on Naxos
       wind bellies black canvas, drives
       Theseus homeward forgetful in triumph.
       The old king, hope destroyed, plunges down
       bequeathes his name to these waters.

Never far from the sea
       where White Star's Britannic,
       liner-turned-hospital-ship,
       went down, holed by a mine

Never far from the sea
       that delivered to Calypso wily Odysseus,
       that swallows refugees and fighting men
       passengers and stokers
       but cast up limp a toddler's body
       Now whatever was his name?

II

Nine ships from Lindos sail off to Troy
        Genoese pirates patrol unruly waters
        young knights serve their year in the galleys

Sulieman's fleet anchors in Kallithéa Bay
        Italian warships bombard entrenchments far inland.
        The Capitoline wolf broods over Mandráki.
        Seaplanes ride at anchor.
        The deer of this island are unique.

Somewhere along the way old Captain Zardis
        puts to sea against advice, is lost in a storm with his son,
        his nephew and the nephew's wife,
        and those are pearls that were their eyes ….

At periscope depth Commander Spanídis
        brings the Papanikolís inshore,
        disembarks commandos, folboat and Lewes bombs,
        tommy-guns and floats, a September mission
        grinding fatigue, abject frustration and deadly fear

A cruise ship dwarfs the Tower of France
        From the moment you step onboard,
        you'll embark on an adventure in more ways than one;
        feel everyday life wash away with the tide

A fisherman from Stegná pays out his nets for barboúni
        there are no apes on the island
        peacocks breed on Filérimos
        the Easter goat rotates on the spit:
        Oh quinquireme of Nineveh never mind the sandalwood,
        just drop us off the wine: we don't trust the water.

ONE MORNING IN HOLY WEEK
For Liana Georgiades

Ding ding dang dang ding dang dong
the church bells batter at the morning air.
Last night's glasses stand unwashed.
A scooter buzzes round the square.

The telly jumbles fashion shows and soaps
with re-run history and news:
jackals hunting in a pack
cut in and out of grainy views

of helicopter gunships;
machine-guns scythe fresh crops in nomansland,
leopards chase down antelopes,
and bombers ply their trade against Japan.

All this between the ads that offer healthier gums
more lustrous hair or perfect skin! Next up
a rhino carcase rots without its horn and after that
a politician struts his catwalk and promises a better life to come...

Press the red button.

The bells that rang out in the breaking light hang stilled.
Someone slams a door.
Out on the balcony two birds quiz for crumbs.
Here on the table
red-dyed hard-boiled eggs nest secure within the Easter bread.

VISITING FAMILY GRAVES
In memory of David Watker

Good Friday, and the national flag is flying at half mast.
The blazon azure, four bars argent;
and a Greek Cross on the canton of the field.
Here for Easter once again, we are visiting family graves.
breathing the waft of incense under the trees,
squinting when sunlight ricochets off marble.
Families wash down memorials, tend lamps, place wreaths:
photographs propose their version of the dead.

So many years have passed since those few summer weeks
between my marriage and your marriage
when I first came to this island.
How many of those who welcomed me
have died since then, Anastássis... Ioulía... Pavlos... Seva... Costa....

That was the year of the *junta*:
Papadopolous and his cronies put tanks on the streets of Athens
clamped down on beards and mini-skirts
rounded up political opponents
locked up Theodorakis, banned his music:
promised, as strong men always do, a new beginning ...

That was the year of the six-day war,
the year of Sergeant Pepper's Lonely Hearts Club Band,
the year when one man got a new heart
and another, after death, was cryonically preserved...

And that year, the year of your marriage, was also the year of your death.
Before the Christmas lights went up I was standing by your casket.
They'd done their best with the rouge, the white shirt, the neatly knotted tie.
It was, I suppose, a kind and skilful presentation
but you, you were long gone,
had taken up fresh lodgings in the universe of loss and recollection.

I have wondered before, and wonder now again
what markers we should raise, we who remain.
Are graves a mark of good fortune?
Who do they benefit? The living or the dead?
I think of knucklebones turned up by the plough,
a skull dredged up with the harbour's silt
a shoulder blade protruding from the mountain snows
and ash cast to the winds from a grassy knoll…

Some tasks of survival have sought me out.
I have tried to find words of comfort,
chosen cards of condolence.
I have smelled the acrid tang of flux
as a lead-lined coffin was being soldered shut,
have seen plywood and wickerwork consigned to the flames,
I have written and delivered funeral orations,
and read the words of the preacher across an open grave.

I have agreed the settlement of undertakers' bills.

A friend you never met explained it to himself:
'So his memorial is not of brass or stone.
Instead you should check out the regard
and affection of his friends ….
If they're dead too, there's nothing left.'

Illis ipsis mortuis, nil restat, he wrote.
If they're dead too, there's nothing left.

We whom you knew have gone our separate ways,
and I wonder who else will remember you now,
and where they are, and what we could say to each other.
For we live in webs of kinship and friendship
fragile as a spider's work and as easily torn,
unpicked by death or trashed by a moment of carelessness.

So every now and then I take the padded album from its presentation box,
turn the interleaved pages until I find you there,
still doing your best-man's job,
reading out those ribbons of text glued onto Post Office forms…

And you return to me privately then,
just for a moment,
from the land of the dead.

THE TOWER

I would have raised a tower
and had your footprints woven
in the carpet of its winding stair;

I would have built a summerhouse
and laid a floor of flints I'd split myself
and patterned it between with horses' teeth;

I would have sunk a well,
installed a windlass with a leather pail
and I'd have set a mirror in the wounded ash.

I would have dug a pond for lilies and for fish.
There would be water iris there,
yellow and mauve

and underneath the spoil dug out
I would have buried deep the fear
that I might lose your love, and plant a sign:

This is the Dragon's grave.
Our children would have slithered
down its slope on summer picnic trays

and we would walk on paths
of camomile and moss –
now at the fence a group of ramblers pause

with clodded boots and knapsacks.
Sunswept, elderly, with walking poles
their anoraks are orange, red and blue,

three quarters of a leisure-country's flag.
One has a map-case, no-one knows the way.
A younger couple hand in hand pass laughing

through me too: except she feels a chill as if a cloud
has sliced across the sun and turning where he was
finds only unrelenting openness of sky.

AT THE CORNER OF PADRE VARELA

For Sarahy Martinez

While I'm worrying
about tripping over my shoelaces
in the bus,

at the corner of Padre Varela
and Santa Marta

a yellow butterfly comes
sailing brightly
along the river of fumes.

ON THE WAY DOWN TO JERICHO

There was a man asleep in a doorway on the corner of George Street
        and a man passed by with headphones over his ears
        reading something on his phone
        there was a poster that said All Enquiries

There was a man with an orange beard lying on a blue sleeping bag
        outside the Royal Academy of Arts
        there was a protest march going past
        with chants and banners and there was a poster
        because the RA was showing the work of Tacita Dean

There was a man bedded down in a November doorway reading a book
        he said it was by Tom Holt
        he said it was called *In your dreams*

There was a man sitting in an angle of stonework staring straight ahead
        and a young woman came with a box of fries,
        and said would you like some fries? and he thanked her
        there was sauce on the fries
        and a poster that said Congrats Harry and Meghan

On the corner of George Street
        on the way down to Jericho
        there was a man sleeping in the street
        and a poster that said All Enquiries

I MUST HAVE WANTED

I must have wanted the entrance of Hampton Court
and the towers as well, so stood well back
and mum and dad walking ahead
got smaller and smaller inside our Brownie Reflex 127.

Sometimes mum got in close like for the one
of me feeding the pigeons in Trafalgar Square
and I took a good one of her in a summer frock
perched on the edge of a fountain

and then one of the two of them together.
At the Round Pond she took one of me
with my electric boat brand new from Hamleys.
I remember the battery was an Ever Ready

and I was crouching down to let it go
when, just as mum pressed the button,
a little girl got nearly in the way.
She was only trying to get a better view,

but everyone who saw her leaning in at the edge
of the picture had a laugh and asked who she was;
Oh just some little girl, dad said.
They always made a joke of that,

But now I see how she turns a family snap
into a question with no simple answer.
It's the story-writer's age-old prompt:
Tell us who she was. What happens next?

And I see too how it shows the picture's edge
for what it is, the enclosure of a space
contained and somehow safe,
an order both intended and imposed

like the space we let enclose ourselves,
secured as much by mind-set as by walls
and I think of the times across the years
when by accident or welcome

someone or something slipped in so to speak
at the edge, the alarm or apprehension,
the excitement sharp with fear and the sense that
Something new can happen now. And here.

ONE THOUSAND PIECES

City in a landscape it said on the box,
a reliable make but with no straight edges

only a ragged border beyond the suburbs
where a road leads in from the north

and a road leads out to the south
past a church on a hill behind a wall

and a road comes in from the east
and another goes out to the west

where men in chains
broke rock in quarries

and when it was done I counted the pieces
up to a thousand, one by one: there were none left over

so I stroked the surface as if a gentle massage
could merge them together, make a continuous map

where I could step over garbage in backstreets
or saunter, elegant flâneur, along broad avenues.

I let my fingers brush through painted swirls of trees,
touch bell-towers, tenements, the mansions of the rich,

trace out the bus routes, dawdle in public gardens
with grand equestrian monuments to heroes

of a liberating war, where people in singlets
were debating politics or playing chess.

There were sea-defences and a lighthouse:
antique cannon spoke to the threat of invasion.

I was happy enough browsing the bookstalls
and quite contented looking for souvenirs

till I chanced upon a couple sharing a pizza.
She was drinking juice and he had a beer

and there was a waiter watching football on TV.
Without a second thought I beckoned for the bill

and as I paid a thousand pieces blended into one,
one image: a narrow door, a darkened stair,

a room where half undone a painting
stood against the wall — and instead

of clamourous streets the whole now
softer than a pillow, broad as an unmade bed.

THE HOME STRAIGHT

I have known love in the Tuileries Gardens
where fountain-spray broke sunlight into rainbows,
at Benares I watched flames consuming flesh on the ghats.
I saw Visnhnu on his bed of snakes at Kathmandu,
and to the Sikh who examined my eyes
I could truthfully report that I had been
to the Golden Temple at Amritsar,
crossing the causeway long before the siege.

When in Jerusalem I met an Irish priest who demanded:
Have you been to all the holy places?
He seemed so excited to be there, all of a lather,
but we had come a long way from Damascus
and crossing over Jordan
found flashy and finned American cars:
the place seemed most unbiblical to me.
and a frontier ran through the city.

I have an abalone shell from Mendocino,
a bowl of beaten brass from Isfahan,
and a snap of my shadow on Brooklyn bridge.
We once had some Rattenberg glass.
The guide in the mines at Hallein said "Hold on tight!"
and down we went WHEEEE!
into the heart of the mountain.
Is Forster an adequate guide at Marabar?

I should make a bucket list really.
Disneyworld Hong Kong or the Strasbourg Clock?
The temples at Angor Wat or the Sistine Chapel,
Auschwitz or the Galapagos?
Easter Island or the Vietnam Wall,
Japan for the Cherry Blossom or Uluru?
I've missed the Bhuddas at Bamiyam,
but I'd still come back with a story to tell ...
And although I've never been to Arles
more than forty years ago I came across Gauguin
in the Jeu de Paume and more recently
at Calais saw Rodin's Burghers --
not, as he envisaged them, on the steps of the Hotel de Ville,
but on a plinth in a manicured garden:
and that same day under a motorway bridge
met the desperate eyes of refugees.

With the right vaccinations I could go on safari,
sleep under a net in the open
and drink bottled water.
I could shoot lions with a telephoto lens
and digitise elephants bathing.
From a safe unbloodying distance,
I'd watch a leopard running down gazelles,
and you could follow my Instagram spoor ...

Across the field behind our house
our cat lay disembowelled – a fox, we think.
Bats plunge from a cranny under the eaves at dusk:
when they hunt over the pond the water-mirror shatters.
Beyond the fence, ewes dropping lambs
lay banquets of afterbirth for crows.
There's a butterfly caught in a cobweb,
a six-spot ladybird spreads its wings.
I've seen the Hapsburg tombs, but never
the pyramids – is Cairo safe these days?
My granddaughter went on some swings in Rhodes
and then we stood where the Jews were rounded up
and talked about history and I met a man who told me
what he saw happen that terrible day in June.
He drew me a little diagram
and seventy years on the tears came fresh to his eyes.

Early one morning I turned a corner
where the road leads down to Jericho
and saw a man sleeping in a doorway.
There was a number to ring
on a weathered sign that said All Enquiries,
and a fellow walked past wearing glasses
reading a message on his phone –
elsewhere never so convenient or at hand.

Driving south, I saw a line of bare and slender trees
standing like artist's brushes in a row:
Spring, I thought, will dip them into leaves
and they will paint with sunlight ...
Police closed the road at the roundabout
and by the garage opposite. A knot of us stood hatless
when flag-draped coffins were returned from war.
I saw a helter-skelter building in the street.

Now with an ear half open for Cock Robin's song
I watch the winter sunbeams probe a pile of logs
and have an eye ajar lest a solitary beetle cross
the split grain – crack, ridge and furrow – of poplar wood;
and I would like, my love, to hold you once again
and I would say these words to all I ever loved,
that whatever happened next I would hold you again.
And would I could.

For
Isabel, Charlie, and Coralie

John Comino-James was born in Somerset in 1943 and has lived near Thame in Oxfordshire since 1984

He has published numerous books of photographs and his work has been exhibited in Thame, Oxford, London, and Havana.

This his first collection of poems.

Just landed safely In Rhodes, Peacocks, goats and sandalwood, One morning In Holy Week, and *Visiting family graves,* were first published in *In the Land from Under the Sea* (Dewi Lewis Publishing 2020)
On the way down to Jericho was first published in *Somewhere near you* (Truffle Books 2018)

First published in December 2020 by
Truffle Books
Shepherds Close
Kingston Stert
Chinnor
Oxon
OX39 4NL

All rights reserved
Copyright © 2020
John Comino-James

ISBN: 978-0-9523867-5-9

Designed by John Comino-James
Printed by MP Printers (Thame) Ltd